THE
BIG IF...

Merry Christmas '95

Love Snuff x

THE
BIG IF...

Steve Bell

Methuen

For Heather, William, Joey, Paddy and Katherine

This collection first published in Great Britain in 1995
by Methuen London
an imprint of Reed Books Ltd
Michelin House, 81 Fulham Road, London SW3 6RB
and Auckland, Melbourne, Singapore and Toronto

The strips first published in the *Guardian* in 1993,
1994 and 1995

Design and production by Brian Homer
Edited by Steve Bell and Brian Homer

A CIP catalogue record for this book
is available from the British Library
ISBN 0 413 69770 3

Linotronic playout by Image Bureau, Birmingham
Printed and bound in England by Clays Ltd, St Ives plc

Contents

Cast of Characters

John Major

The Iron Lady (retired)

Burglar Bill

The Queen

Bill Clinton

Socks the Cat

Dr Death

Pulp Quango

Kipling

Pope John Paul II

John Smith

**Lilley the Kid
and Wild Bill Haircut**

**The Lone Parent
and Tonto**

Parcelforce Pat

Crazy Hezza

Boris Yeltsin

God

Prince Charles

John the Monkey

Tony Blair

6

The Very Rich Hours of the Duke of Edinburgh 1995

With apologies to the Limbourg Brothers and Jean Colombe

June – July 1993

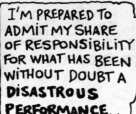

THIS IS SO **UNFAIR!**

GO NOW

SACK THE TURNIP

I'M PREPARED TO ADMIT MY SHARE OF RESPONSIBILITY FOR WHAT HAS BEEN WITHOUT DOUBT A **DISASTROUS** PERFORMANCE...

...THAT'S WHY I'M PUNISHING MYSELF BY PROMOTING **FATTY, OILY, DEADWOOD** AND **GUMBUM!**

WHY DO THEY **HATE ME SO??**

BRING BACK OLD BIG 'EAD

OL'BIG 'EAD WE SAY **DRY NER OUT** AND **WHEEL HER IN**

YOUNG MAN - YOU'RE A DISGRACE!!

OH NO! IT'S MY **WORST NIGHTMARE!**

BIG 'EAD

I OUGHT TO **KICK YOUR BOTTOM,** YOUNG MAN!

YOU'VE BEEN LETTING **FOREIGNERS** SCORE **IN OUR GOAL!!**

IT'S OUR BOYS' JOB TO SCORE IN **OUR GOAL!**

BRAVO MA'AM!

YOUNG MAN - THE SECRET IS - DON'T ALLOW **FOREIGN BASTARDS** ANYWHERE NEAR **OUR GOALMOUTH**

HAVE YOU **GOT THAT?**

BIG 'EAD

GUMBUM - IMAGINE I'M A **FOREIGN BASTARD** - I WANT YOU TO HURL YOUR- SELF AT MY FEET

WITH PLEASURE MA'AM!

...THEN FLING THE BALL IN YOUR OWN **NET** AND A QUICK "V" TO THE FANS!

WATCH THESE **SKILLS** YOUNG MAN - - YOU MIGHT **LEARN SOMETHING**

I HOLD MY LEG LIKE THIS AND **HOWL** A BIT

THEN THE COACH BRINGS ON THE **VODKA BOTTLE...**

SNATCH

...AND I GET UP AGAIN. **TRY IT YOURSELF!**

YOU MEDIA BASTARDS ARE BEING **TOO HARD** ON THE BOY!

– 11·6·3213 –

IT'S NOT THAT HE'S A USELESS LITTLE TOSSER WITH **NO BOTTOM**....

WAH!

...IT'S JUST HE'S GOT A SLIGHT **REFUELLING PROBLEM**, HAVEN'T YOU, YOUNG MAN?

© Steve Bell '93

COULD YOU EXPLAIN WHAT YOU MEAN BY "**NO BOTTOM**"??

I'M GLAD YOU ASKED ME THAT QUESTION YOUNG MAN...

– 12·6·3214 –

"**BOTTOM**" IS WHAT YOU GET FROM YEARS OF EXPERIENCE IN THE GAME. IT'S LIKE A **SOLID FOUNDATION** ....FEEL THAT!

WHEREAS WITH 'IM... 'ERE LAD – SHOW US WHAT'S IN YOUR **UNDERPANTS**!

ROLLED UP SOCKS! SEE?!!

© Steve Bell 1993

14·6·3215 –

– © Steve Bell 1993 –

15·6·3216 –

– © Steve Bell 1993 –

10

11

LOOK SIR BILL — THE **FACT OF THE MATTER** IS: YOU CAN'T JUST **WALK IN HERE** WITH A **WHEELBARROW** FULL OF **DOSH** AND DEMAND A **PEERAGE!**...

...IT'S A **CRIMINAL OFFENCE**, AND BESIDES, YOU CAN'T EXPECT TO **BUY INFLUENCE** IN THE CONSERVATIVE PARTY!

NORMAN — I'LL LET THE MONEY **PUT YOU STRAIGHT**

SIR BILL DOESN'T WANT **INFLUENCE!**

HE DOESN'T WANT TO **BUY AMENDMENTS** TO **LEGISLATION!**

HE DOESN'T WANT TO **FLOG BOOZE** OR **FAGS!**

HE DOESN'T WANT TO **SMASH STRIKES** OR EMPLOY A **DIRTY TRICKS UNIT!**

HE JUST WANTS TO **SIT IN THE HOUSE OF LORDS** AND GET ON WITH HIS **BURGLING!**

LORD ROTHERMERE OF THE **MOUTHPIECE** LORD STERLING OF **RORORO**, LORD KING OF **TRICKS** AND LORD HANSON OF **LUNGSHADOW**.....

YOU MAY **SWAP YOUR HATS** AND BOW **THREE TIMES**. I NOW PRONOUNCE THIS MAN **LORD BILL OF SCRUBS!**

YOU MAY **KISS** THE **DEAD SHEEP**......**NEXT!**

LADY BOTTERLEY'S MOTHER

REPEAT AFTER ME:

"I CAR, I CAR, I RALEIGH RALEIGH CAR!!"

"I CAR, I CAR, I RALEIGH RALEIGH CAR!"....YES, BUT WHAT DOES IT **MEAN** MOTHER?

IT'S NOT WHAT IT **MEANS**, IT'S THAT IT **SOUNDS CLASSY**, YOU SILLY **TROLLOP!!** NOW — TELL **MAJORS** TO GIVE ME A **SHOVE!**

Lady Botterley's Mother

"I CAR, I CAR, I RALEIGH RALEIGH CAR"!!

WHY DOES THIS **PLANK** MAKE ME FEEL **SO ALIVE?**

THA'MUN TEK HEED O' YON **PLANK**, LADY BOTTERLEY

COULDST CATCH A SPLINTER WHICH WOULD **RIP THI' PANTS CLEAN OFF!!**

13

Lady Botterley's Mother

"I CAR I CAR! I RALEIGH RALEIGH CAR!"

...AND WILL THIS EGG BECOME A **LITTLE CHICK** IN TIME?

NAY LASS, FOR I MUN **SHOOT IT** 'AFORE IT'S 'ATCHED....

..TO CUT COSTS AND SAVE ON **FEED** AN' **BEATERS!** HAST THA' MET MA **PET RAT NORMAN?**

THE DARLING! MAY I HOLD HIM?

MMMM— HE HAS SUCH **LOVELY SLIPPERY FUR!**

MAJORS! ISN'T THAT AWFULLY **DANGEROUS??**

NAY LASS— IT'S PERFECTLY **SAFE**... ...THERE'S NO RISK OF PROSECUTION, AND WHAT'S MORE: THERE'S A **BLOODY GOOD RETURN** ON IT !!

A **CHEQUE** FOR **SIXTY MILLION DRACHMA!** HOW DOES HE DO IT?

AYE LASS! ..BUT IT'S A **CHEQUE** FOR **3 MILLION HONG KONG DOLLARS!**

...AND IT'S ALL FOR **THEE** LASS... FOR I COULD ALLUS TELL FROM THE **FIRST MOMENT** I CLAPPED EYES ON THEE....

THAT THA WERT **DYIN' FOR A BUNG!** ...AND WHAT A **BIG** ONE!

NEW HATS! ELOCUTION LESSONS FOR **T'ENTIRE POPULATION!** IT'S ALL FOR THEE, LASS! SAY **"THANKYOU NORMAN!"**

THANKYOU NORMAN — I RALEIGH CAR!!

THANKS TO HUGH.

15

BY THE RIGHT: QUICK MARCH : BEAT THAT DRUM!!

WE'LL SHOW THOSE CHEESERS AND SQUEAKERS WHO'S BOSS IN THIS COMMUNITY!!

BOOM BOOM BOOM BOOM BOOM!

BOOM BOOM BOOM BOOM BOOM BOOM BOOM BOOM BOOM

♫ THE FLEA COLLAR MY FATHER WORE...

REMEMBER LYMESWOLD NO CHEESE HERE

©Steve Bell '93

THE FLEA·COLLAR MY FATHER WORE... HEY!!

SECURITY! SECURITY!! DID YOU SEE THAT? THE SQUEAKERS THREW CHEESE AT ME! AARRRGHH!

SECURITY! WHERE THE HELL IS SECURITY?

REMEMBER LYMESWOLD NO CHEESE HERE

STAKE OUT THAT HOLE UNTIL FURTHER NOTICE! I'VE GOT TO GO AND LIE DOWN!!

©Steve Bell 1993

10.7.3238

Lady Botterley

DOODLE DOO A COCK!

12.7.3239

MMM.... I FEEL THE PLANKS.... ...THEIR WARMTH... ...HOW THEY ALL FIT TOGETHER....

...TO MAKE A WHOLE SHED.... I FEEL.... GOOD GRIEF!!

©Steve Bell 1993

DIDST THA' MISS ME, LASS?

Lady Botterley

WHY ARE YOU DRESSED AS A CABBAGE?

I AM THE JANUARY KING! WILT THA' BE MA SPROUT?

OH GOD!

WE CAN LIVE IN T'SHED FOR EVER AND EVER! I CAN PUT A SACK OVER ME 'EAD AN' THA' CANST SWEEP UP AFTER ME!

OWOOO!! WOOF! WOOF!

JOHN.... I THINK YOU MAY BE IN NEED OF CAR!!

©Steve Bell 1993

16

17

August – September 1993

MI6
TIME: 23·55
TEMP: 15°
FUZZY
ACTIVITY: NORMAL

SHOME JOINT THEY GOT HERE!

IV

SHOMETIME'SH YOU GOTTA TAKE THE BULL BY THE HORNSH, WALK IN THE FRONT DOOR..

NO HAWKERS
NO CIRCULARS
NO MILKMEN
NO COMMUNIST
NO FUZZIES

...AND ASHK A SHTRAIGHT QUESTION: WHERE ARE YOU HOLDING GENERAL GORDON??

ARE YOU A SPERM DONOR?

THISH ISH CRAZY—— I ASHK YOU WHERE YOU'RE HOLDING GENERAL GORDON AND YOU ASHK ME IF I'M A SHPERM DONOR!

SURE

I WANT EXPLANATIONSH NOW!! MI6-WHO? HOW? WHAT? WHY??

SIDDOWN! YOU SEE THIS BLOOD STAINED UNION JACK?

YOU MEAN..?

YEP! FROM IT WE'VE ISOLATED THE D.N.A. OF GENERAL GORDON. WE JUST NEED THE RIGHT SPERM DONOR

...AND WE CAN REPOPULATE THE EARTH WITH IMPERIAL ROLE MODELS

FETCH ME A BUCKET AND A COPY OF JANE'SH FIGHTING SHIPSH!

I SAY— IS THIS YOUR FAMOUS SWEDISH "SMORGASBORD"?

NO

IT'S A DISH OF COLD PEAS.

WHO ARE YOU?

I'M A NOBEL PRIZE HOT CERTAINTY!!

WHICH NOBEL PRIZE ARE YOU IN LINE FOR?

THE ONE FOR A LIFETIME'S ACHIEVEMENT OF UNPARALLELED FUTILITY AND USELESSNESS *

* HOLDER: MILTON FRIEDMAN

HEY! THAT'S MY PRIZE!

I TELL YOU WHAT —WE'LL EAT PEAS FOR IT! THE ONE WHO EATS THE LAST PEA WINS THE NOBEL PRIZE!

21

DO WE COUNT **BLACK ONES??**

DON'T **STARE AT ME** LIKE THAT!

WHY ARE YOU STARING LIKE THAT?

BECAUSE YOU'RE **DOOMED!**

I'M NOT **DOOMED.** I JUST HAVE A SLIGHT **PRESENTATIONAL PROBLEM**

YOU'LL NEVER GET **MY JOB,** DEATH!!

I DON'T **WANT YOUR** JOB!....

"I'M **OUT OF** POLITICS - THERE'S NO AMBITION LEFT IN ME."

WHY IS THAT **SMOKE** COMING OUT OF YOUR **HABIT?**

BECAUSE MY **PANTS ARE ON FIRE!!**

LOOK! BEHIND YOU!!

OH **NO!** I'VE GOT THE **PENULTIMATE PEA!** THAT MEANS **YOU** GET THE **LAST PEA** AND THE **NOBEL PRIZE!**

GRRRRRR!! I FEEL SO CROSS I COULD **CLUB** A BIG-EYED BABY SEAL!!

WITH APOLOGIES TO INGMAR BERGMAN

DUCKLANDS:

23·8·3257·

SIGH

FOR SALE

BIJOU GUANO REPOSITORY

I'M TIRED OF THIS **ARTIFICIAL EXISTENCE** ....

©Steve Bell 1993

I NEED A **USEFUL HOBBY** THAT'LL GET ME OUT OF THIS CRAP **HOLE**

HOW ABOUT **FISHING** .... FOR A **PLUMP THAMES SALMON**?

I'M NOT DIVING INTO **THAT** CRAP HOLE!

GO ON - A BIT OF EXERCISE WILL DO YOU **GOOD**!

24·8·3258·

GO ON! IT'S NOW OR NEVER!!

SEEN ANY **SALMON** YET?

NO, BUT I'M GETTING WARM - HERE'S A **TESCO'S CARRIER BAG**!

©Steve Bell 1993

BLIMEY! IS THAT A **SALMON**?

25·8·3258·

I THINK I'VE **SEEN ONE**! A REALLY **BIG FISH**!! I'M **NOT JOKING**!

ARE YOU A **SALMON**?

ARE YOU A **PHØTØGRÅPHER**? I WAS **PRØMISED** AN **EXCLUSIVE TELEVISION DEAL** TO SWIM UP THIS **SHJITHØL**!!

©Steve Bell 1993·

BLIMEY! WHAT A **WHOPPER**!

HJELLØ! PHØTØGRÅPHER? QUICK! TAKE MY **PICTURE**!!·

...THEN I'LL HAVE **FJÜLFJILLED** MY **CØNTRÅCT** AND I CAN **FJØERK** OFF BACK TO THE **FJØRDS**!

26·8·3260·

IS **THÅT** A PHOTØGRÅPHER?

NO - IT'S AN **ENORMOUS POOP SLICK**!

THE FISH HAS **FAINTED**!

SWOON

©Steve Bell '93

Ottober — December 1993

31

32

DEMOCRACY IN ACTION

MORNING IN BLACKPOOL:
MABEL — HAVE YOU SEEN THE **VARNISH**?

6·10·3289 · © Steve Bell 1993

I THINK IT'S IN THE **GREY CASE** WITH THE **BELLADONNA**, FRANK

SHLUP
SLOP
GLUG
GLUG
SPLOT

DEMOCRACY IN ACTION

7·10·3290

WHAT ARE YOU GOING TO DO WHEN **MARGARET** COMES ONTO THE PLATFORM?

WELL.... I'M GOING TO **JIBBER**, AND THEN I'M GOING TO **WHOOP** AND **SHRIEK**!

© Steve Bell 1993

WHAT ABOUT **YOU**, DEAR?

I'M SIMPLY GOING TO **BARK LIKE A DOG**!

DEMOCRACY IN ACTION

8·10·3291

I MAY NOT LOOK MUCH **NOW**.....

...BUT WHEN I GET ON THAT CONFERENCE FLOOR I'M LIKE A **WILDBEAST**...

...WITH A **VORACIOUS APPETITE** FOR BLOODY LUMPS OF REACTIONARY **RAW MEAT** WHICH THE LEADERSHIP IS OBLIGED TO TOSS ME ON PAIN OF **HORRIBLE DEATH**!

GOOD MORNING SIR! THE BEST OF LUCK WITH YOUR SPEECH!!

© Steve Bell 1993

DEMOCRACY IN ACTION

9·10·3292

TRAIN'S LATE! TYPICAL BRITISH RAILWAYS!

IT'S DISGRACEFUL! WE TORIES SHOULD **DO SOMETHING** ABOUT IT!!

© Steve Bell 1993

THAT'S WHY I'M GOING TO GO INTO THIS TOILET....

Gentlemen

...AND **HANG MYSELF NOW!** GOODBYE DAPHNE. THERE IS A HAPPY LAND....

·11·10·3293

I THINK WE SHOULD BE TOLD

ABOLISH HOPE

© Steve Bell 1993—

MISTER HOWARD...

..COULD YOU PRONOUNCE THE FOLLOWING PHRASES?

"LLLOTS AND LLLOTS OF LLLLOATHSOME LLLAGS; LLLLLIMITLESS UNEM-PLLLOYED PEEPILLL"

I THINK WE SHOULD BE TOLD

12·10·3294

ABOLISH HOPE

MISTER LILLEY...

AVEZ-VOUS UN MAISON EN FRANCE? CLAIMEZ-VOUS LE REPAIR SUBSIDY?

..ÊTES-VOUS DANS UN RELATIONSHIP AVEC MICHEL PORTILLO?

ABOLISH HOPE

© Steve Bell 1993—

I THINK WE SHOULD BE TOLD

13·10·3295·

ABOLISH HOPE

MR HURD...

..DO YOU PREFER CANE, SLIPPER OR LEATHER STRAP??

© Steve Bell 1993

MISTER CLARKE.....

ABOLISH HOPE

ARE YOU, OR HAVE YOU EVER BEEN A TRAIN SPOTTER?

ABOLISH HOPE

I THINK WE SHOULD BE TOLD

14·10·3296

ABOLISH HOPE

MRS THATCHER...

..WOULD YOU LIKE A PROPER DRINK?

© Steve Bell '93.

ABOLISH HOPE

I THINK WE SHOULD BE TOLD

ABOLISH HOPE

MR FOWLER...

WHAT'S THE GOING-RATE FOR TABLING A QUESTION IN THE HOUSE OF COMMONS?

ABOLISH HOPE

YOU WERE IN GROUP 4 — COULD YOU LOOK AFTER MY WATCH FOR A FEW DAYS?

ABOLISH HOPE

15·10·3297

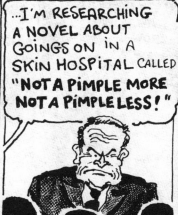

I THINK WE SHOULD BE TOLD

ABOLISH HOPE

MR ARCHER...

...I'M RESEARCHING A NOVEL ABOUT GOINGS ON IN A SKIN HOSPITAL CALLED "NOT A PIMPLE MORE NOT A PIMPLE LESS!"

...COULD YOU TELL ME WHICH IS THE SPOTTIEST — YOUR BACK OR YOUR TONGUE??

16·10·3298

ANTIQUES ROADSHOW

18·10·3299

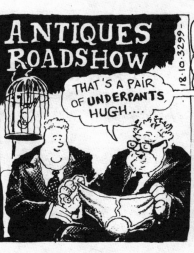

THAT'S A PAIR OF UNDERPANTS HUGH....

...WHAT ARE CALLED "MARKS AND SPENCERS AERTEX"....SEE THE HOLES IN NEAT ROWS....

...AND THERE'S THE LABEL, SEE THE WORDS "ST. MICHAEL"..

NOW LET'S SEE IF WE CAN FIND THE 'SKIDMARK'

St Michael MADE IN THE UK UK LARGE

Roadtiques Antshow

19·10·3300

NOW THIS LOOKS LIKE SOMETHING SPECIAL!

AS I THOUGHT.... ...THIS IS QUITE QUITE SPLENDID...

...IT'S AN ALTOGETHER UNIQUE SPECIMEN.. ...I'LL JUST ADJUST THE HEADPIECE

LOOK AT THE EYEBALLS LOOK AT THE LITTLE FLECKS OF FOAM — THIS IS A LATE 20TH CENTURY BARKING BRASS BAT!

-©Steve Bell 1993-

Antroad's Showtique

·20·10·3301·

LOOK AT THOSE EYEBALLS! QUITE QUITE SPLENDID!

...NOW I'LL JUST SEE IF I CAN WIND HER UP....

©Steve Bell '93

I'LL JUST WHISPER "ULTIMATE TRIUMPH OF SOCIALIST INTERNATIONALISM" "T. AND G. FOR ME!" INTO HERE....

...SEE: STARTING TO FOAM..... NO! G. AND T! G. AND T!!

ANTIQUES ROADSHOW

DO YOU REMEMBER...

..."NOT ONE FISH"?

STAND BACK HUGH!

21·10·3302·

CRAZY, HAPPY DAYS! ROWF! ROWF!! RRRROWF!!

"GREAT CORN FROM HEARTS OF OAK DOTH FLOW!!" YIP! YIP!!

©Steve Bell 1993

DID YOU KNOW I ENDED WORLD AGGRESSION IN 1982?

I STOPPED WORLD AGGRESSIVE BEHAVIOUR IN ITS TRACKS IN 1982!

22·10·3303·

I INVENTED THE FOAM IN LYONS MAID ICE CREAM, THE PERSONAL COMPUTER AND THE TELEGRAPH POLE...

...I NEVER TRUSTED THAT GUMMER FARTHER THAN I COULD THROW HIM!

©Steve Bell 1993

"WHEN ONE IS BRASS ONE IS WITHOUT MUCK"

·23·10·3304·

DID I EVER HAVE AN ORGASM, JENNY? IT WAS AN ELEVEN YEAR MUTUAL ORGASM FOR MYSELF, THE PARTY AND THE COUNTRY....

...BUT AT THE END OF THE DAY I LIKE NOTHING BETTER THAN TO SETTLE DOWN WITH A SCOTCH, AN ELEPHANT TRANQUILISER AND A 'BEAVIS AND BUTTHEAD' VIDEO....

©Steve Bell '93

I WAS BETRAYED BY MY HAIRDRESSER YOU KNOW.....

BY GOSH! I FEEL **DANGEROUS** TODAY.....

DINGALING A LING

...I FEEL LIKE GOING OUT AND **STORMING** SOMETHING !!

...BUT FIRST I MUST **FOLD** MY PYJAMAS

-25·10·3305-

©Steve Bell'93

WATCH OUT BRITAIN— I'M IN A **STORMING** MOOD!

-26·10·3306-

MARGARET—ABOUT TODAY'S **SHADOW CABINET** MEETING...

...I WANT TO SEE AT LEAST **SEVEN AND A HALF WOMEN** THERE...

...AND I WANT EVERYBODY TO BRING THEIR **PETS**

©Steve Bell 1993

PRESCOTT— WHY ON EARTH HAVE YOU BROUGHT **TWO TORTOISES**

23·10·3307

THE RULES ARE PERFECTLY CLEAR: **ONE MAN ONE PET**......

©Steve Bell'93

...I BEG YOUR PARDON— **ONE MEMBER ONE PET.** NOW, HAVE THE PETS ANYTHING THEY WISH TO RAISE?

No...**NO!** I'M AFRAID I'M **SICK AND TIRED** OF HEARING ABOUT THE **BUDGIE!**

IS THIS **YOUR FERRET**, MARGARET?

23·10·3308

VERY FETCHING LITTLE CHAP! WHAT DO YOU **FEED HIM ON?**

LIVE CHICKENS AND WEETABIX, JOHN

NOW — WOULD YOU ALL LIKE TO SEE **MY PET?**

OOH YES!

YES PLEASE JOHN!

YES!

I THINK YOU'LL ALL AGREE—SHE'S A RATHER SPECIAL **BABY ELEPHANT!**

©Steve Bell'93

...SO I THOUGHT IT'S TIME WE CHANGED OUR NAME TO THE 'PEOPLES' PETS PARTY'

LIKE IT!

MMM

29·10·3309

ON THE ECONOMY — WE'RE NOT JUST GOING TO TALK ABOUT CHANGE...

© Steve Bell '93

...WE'RE GOING TO COLLECT MILK BOTTLE TOPS!

OH NO!!

SPLORP

OH BOTHER!

OH LORD!

30·10·3310

PENNY FOR THE GUY?

— © Steve Bell 1993 —

ROCKET UP YOUR BOTTOM?

LET'S FACE IT NORMAN — WE'RE IN A HOLE!

1·11·3311

WE MUST APPLY MAJOR'S FIRST LAW OF POLITICAL DYNAMICS...

"WHEN YOU'RE IN A HOLE DIG AN EVEN DEEPER ONE. THERE'S NO PREDICAMENT THAT CAN'T BE MADE TO APPEAR CONSIDERABLY BETTER BY COMPARISON WITH A REMARKABLY WORSE ONE!"

© Steve Bell '93

LET'S GO DOWN TO THE BUNKER AND DISCUSS THE JUBILEE LINE EXTENSION!

WE ARE HERE IN THIS CRUMBLING HOLE UNDERNEATH DOWNING ST. OUR FRIENDS ARE HERE IN CANARY WHARF.....

2·11·33·2

...THE JUBILEE EXTENSION WILL ENABLE US TO VISIT OUR FRIENDS WHEN WE'VE SHUT ALL THE OTHER RAILWAYS, AND THE ROADS ARE CHOKED. ANY QUESTIONS? ANYBODY GOT ANY MONEY FOR THE METER?

© Steve Bell '93

BASICS CASSIDY

AND THE

MOONDANCE KID

LILLEY THE KID AND WILD BILL HAIRCUT

WHAT'S UP LIL?

LOOKS TO ME LIKE SOME KINDA SILVER SPOON! LOOKEE — THERE'S WRITIN' ON IT!

IT SAYS: "COURTESY OF THE BRITISH TAXPAYER" THIS CAN ONLY MEAN ONE THING.....

...THE LONE PARENT AND TONTO ARE BACK IN TOWN!

HI HO GIRO AND AWAY!

15·11·3323

© Steve Bell 1993

THE LONE PARENT AND TONTO

CHECK OUT THOSE TRACKS, TONTO....

UG!

SEE — UM COUNCIL SHACK WITH UM FEATHER BED AND UM FREE LUNCH, MUM, — YUM!

NOT SO FAST, LONE PARENT! REACH FOR THE SKY!!

OH NO! IT'S LILLEY THE KID!.. —AND WILD BILL HAIRCUT!

LONE PARENT — WE GOT WORK FOR YOU! — YOU RUN TO YOUR GRANPAW'S CHILD —AFORE I BLOW YER NAPPY AWAY!

HAR HAR!

-16·11·3324-

© Steve Bell '93

LILLEY THE KID AND WILD BILL HAIRCUT

LONE PARENT — WHAT YOUR CHILD NEEDS IS AN ADULT ETHNICALLY UNCHALLENGED RIGHT MALE AS A ROLE MODEL....

INDEED, KEMO SABAY!

SEE — HE'S ALREADY RES- -PONDING TO MY INFLUENCE BY SHOWING ME RESPECT!

YOU'RE RIGHT, KEMO SABAY!

...I WANT TO BE LIKE YOU, KEMO SABAY — -I WANT TO BE ABLE TO LIE, CHEAT, STEAL...

...AND GENERALLY TREAT THE HUMAN RACE LIKE AN EVIL SMELLING PILE OF KEMO SABAY, KEMO SABAY!

-17·11·3325-

© Steve Bell 1993

BASICS CASSIDY AND THE MOONDANCE KID

Y'HEAR ANYTHANG, MOONY?

AH KIN HEAR A TRAIN FULL O' DOUGH, BASICS!

ARE YOU READY TO KILL THE TRAIN?

YUP!

O.K.! LET'S EAT THE DOUGH!

-18·11·3326-

© Steve Bell 1993

42

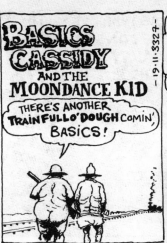

43

45

January – February 1994

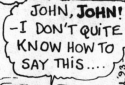

53

DIPLOMACY AT LARGE

- 12-11- 332-1 -

JOHN – WE HAVE A **HISTORIC OPPORTUNITY** HERE...

ADAMS AND THE REP-UBLICANS WANT A **SETTLEMENT**, BUT WHAT THEY NEED IS SOME SORT O' **FACE-SAVIN' FORMULA**

FACE-SAVING FORMULA?? HMMM....LET ME THINK....

© Steve Bell 1993

I KNOW! HE CAN HAVE "I'M A SORRY **IRISH FAILURE**" TATTOOED ON HIS BOTTOM!

I'M IN A HOLE, BUT I FIND THAT SPIDER **STRANGELY INSPIRATIONAL**...

- 18-11- 3322 -

GRUNT

CLAMBER

HE BUMPS HIS HEAD, FALLS, THEN **TRIES AGAIN**......

..FOR, IF AT FIRST YOU DON'T SUCCEED....

..**TRY FAILING AGAIN**....

..THEN GET THE **BBC** TO TALK UP YOUR **SUCCESS**!

© Steve Bell 1993

NNNGH........ I THINK I'M GETTING A **HEADACHE**

- 10-1- 3358 -

THE MOST POWERFUL CAT ON EARTH

IT'S BEEN **THREE WHOLE HOURS** SINCE I HAD A **BIMBO!**

© Steve Bell 94.

SECURITY?

THE MOST POWERFUL CAT ON EARTH

LIMO ME A BIMBO NOW!!

THE MOST POWERFUL CAT ON EARTH

MMMMM... MY HEAD FEELS BETTER NOW..... WHERE DID YOU SAY YOU WERE FROM, HONEY?

I DIDN'T SAY ANYTHING, SOCKS

- 11-11- 3359 -

YOU'RE **CUTE**, SUGAR — PEEL ME A PRAWN NOW!

SOCKS?!?!

OH NO!! IT'S **WANDSWORTH!** GET OUTA HERE!!!

SOCKS – I WANT TO TALK TO YOU ABOUT **THE FAMILY**....

© Steve Bell 1994

55

BORIS — I'D LIKE YOU TO MEET **SOCKS**, MY LEADING POLICY ADVISER

BORIS: SOCKS — SOCKS: BORIS

OK — LET'S APPLAUD OURSELVES FOR THE CAMERA!

BILL, SOCKS — I'D LIKE YOU TO MEET **BOOTS**, MY AMAZING DANCING BEAR!

© Steve Bell '94

THIS IS **BOOTS**, MY DANCING BEAR; — BOOTS: BILL, BILL: BOOTS, BOOTS: SOCKS, SOCKS: BOOTS

LET'S BREAK FOR **MUTUAL APPLAUSE!**

© Steve Bell 1994

WHAT DO WE DO **NOW?**

LET'S ALL AGREE **HERE AND NOW** TO TARGET ALL OUR NUCLEAR MISSILES ON THE GROWING **WORLD FISH THREAT!!**

SOCKS! WHAT A FABULOUS IDEA!

THIS IS **WONDERFUL!** THIS IS **STATESMANSHIP!**

WE DE·TARGET YOU; YOU DE·TARGET US!!

....AND THEN WE TARGET THE **COLD·BLOODED SCALY THREAT** THAT **LURKS** BENEATH THE WAVES!!

© Steve Bell '94

BOOTS WILL NOW PERFORM **AUTHENTIC RUSSIAN FOLKDANCE** FOR YOU!

A·ONE·TWO· THREE·FOUR....

© Steve Bell 1994

....WO·WO..... .....YAY·YAY.....

....HITCH- -HIKER!!

57

TAKE ONE DEAD RUBBER CHICKEN AND ONE BAG OF BONES...

IT'S THE GALOOPING GOURMET FROM MARS!

STEP ONE: LIGHTLY MIND-MELD WITH THE RUBBER CHICKEN...

STEP TWO: SHAKE THE BAG OF BONES VIGOROUSLY!...

STEP THREE: BORROW SOME HARD CURRENCY AND VISIT MACDONALDS

© Steve Bell 1994

PARP PARP

MAN FROM MARS — DO YOU REALLY THINK WE CAN SELL THIS "DRIVE WHERE YOU WANT" SLOGAN TO THE RUSSIAN PEOPLE?

PARP PARP

YOU BET!

BORIS — WHAT DO YOU THINK?

I THINK I NEED A STIFF "CUP OF TEA"!

© Steve Bell 94

PARP PARP

BORIS — I THINK YOU SHOULD KNOW — THIS GUY IS DANGEROUS!

PARP

HAS HE GOT ANY TANKS TO STAND ON?

NO, BUT THAT DOESN'T MAKE HIM ANY LESS DANGEROUS!

© Steve Bell 94.

NO TANKS — NO WORRIES! ...GLUG...

PARP PARP

SOCKS! I'M WORRIED! I NEED YOUR HELP!

BOOTS! IT'S DIFFICULT — I'M UP TO MY EYES IN "WHITEWATERGATE"

© Steve Bell '94

IT'S "MAN FROM MARS" — HE'S CAUSING HAVOC!

JUST DO EXACTLY AS HE TELLS YOU, AND YOU CAN'T GO WRONG!

BUT HE'S NOTHING BUT A PSYCHO-PATHIC ALIEN JOYRIDER!

LISTEN, HAIRYASS! DO AS HE SAYS OR YOU CAN KISS SIBERIO-DISNEY GOODBYE!!!

58

February – March 1994

HHHHHHHH.... ...HHHHHHHHH....

HHHHAS-BEEN'S HALF HOUR!

CLOSE THE BOOK; PUT IT ON THE SHELF!

15·2·3389

WALK DOWN THE ROW OF SHELVES; PICK ANOTHER HEFTY BOOK; LOOK SERIOUS....

© Steve Bell '94

..WALK TOWARDS THE CAMERA HOLDING THE OPEN BOOK... CUT! CUT!! YOUR HEAD'S STARTING TO SHRINK! MAKE UP!!! EMERGENCY!!!

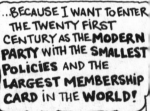

CLAUSE FOUR: THERE IT IS — ON THE MEMBERSHIP CARD

I PUT IT THERE; NOW I WANT TO TAKE IT AWAY AGAIN ....

16·2·3390

TIME-LIFE BOOK OF GRAVITAS

..BECAUSE I THINK, LIKE ME IT'S A WASTE OF SPACE. I WANT TO REPLACE IT WITH CLAUSE FOUR THOU-SAND FOUR HUNDRED AND FORTY FOUR, WHICH I'VE JUST THIS MINUTE MADE UP......

..BECAUSE I WANT TO ENTER THE TWENTY FIRST CENTURY AS THE MODERN PARTY WITH THE SMALLEST POLICIES AND THE LARGEST MEMBERSHIP CARD IN THE WORLD!

© Steve Bell 1994

17·2·3391-

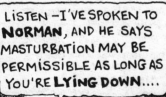

Panel 1: FLYING BISHOP SPEAKING: HOW CAN I BE OF ASSISTANCE?

Panel 2: BISHOP — I NEED TO KNOW: IS MASTURB-ATION WRONG? HOW FIRMLY SHOULD WE CONDEMN IT?

Panel 3: IT'S A TICKLISH ISSUE. THERE ARE DEFINITE DRAWBACKS TO THE SIN OF ONAN. HOW TO HANDLE IT — THERE'S THE RUB...... WE'LL BE WITH YOU IN A COUPLE OF SHAKES!!

Panel 4: D.F.E. TO FLYING BISHOPS; D.F.E. TO FLYING BISHOPS!

Panel 5: D.F.E. THIS IS FLYING BISHOPS; WHAT'S YOUR PROBLEM?

Panel 6: FLYING BISHOPS: THIS IS D.F.E: I WANT YOU TO COME DOWN HARD ON SEX IN SCHOOLS!

Panel 7: D.F.E.: THIS IS FLYING BISHOPS: — YOU SAUCY CREATURE!!

24·2·3397

PATTEN - LUST FOR PRUDERY

FLYING BISHOPS: THIS IS D.F.E!

THE TEACHER/PERVERTS ARE CLOSING IN ON ME! I NEED YOUR SUPPORT NOW, BISHOPS!!

D.F.E: THIS IS FLYING BISHOPS. WHAT EXACTLY DO YOU REQUIRE?

I WANT A BIBLICAL CONDEMN-ATION OF MASTURBATION, AND I WANT IT NOW, IN NO UNCERTAIN TERMS!

RRRRR

PATTEN - LUST FOR PRUDERY

FLYING BISHOPS? THIS IS D.F.E... HURRY UP!!

...THE TEACHER/PERVERTS ARE ALMOST ON ME!

D.F.E: THIS IS FLYING BISHOPS: — WE'VE GOT YOU A BIBLICAL CONDEMNATION OF MASTURBATION!

HAVE YOU GOT A PENCIL?

HANG ON — THERE'S ONE STICKING UP MY ARSE!

TAKE THIS DOWN: GENESIS: CHAPTER 38, VERSE 9....

"AND IT CAME TO PASS, WHEN HE WENT IN UNTO HIS BROTHER'S WIFE, THAT HE SPILLED IT ON THE GROUND LEST THAT HE SHOULD GIVE SEED TO HIS BROTHER. AND THE THING WHICH HE DID DISPLEASED THE LORD: WHEREFORE HE SLEW HIM ALSO." WILL THAT DO YOU??

NOW HEAR THIS, TEACHER/PERVERTS I WANT THE WORDS "WANKING KILLS" PRINTED AT THE BOTTOM OF EVERY BLACKBOARD IN THE LAND!!

RRRR

WHAT'S GOING ON??

WE'VE HAD A TIP-OFF — IT'S GUMMER'S FIRST CATHOLIC COMMUNION

SO WHAT? SO HE'S NOT USING WAFERS....

...HE'S USING HAMBURGERS MADE FROM 100% SELLAFIELD BEEF!!

...AND HE'S DOING IT IN LATIN!

I PROTEST! WOMEN PRIESTS ARE AN ABOMINATION!

ANGLICANISM HAS BECOME LITTLE MORE THAN A SECT!

NOT ONLY AM I TURNING CATHOLIC IN THE STRONGEST POSSIBLE TERMS....

SHAKE SHAKE

...I AM ALSO GOING TO WEAR DRAG UNTIL THE CHURCH COMES TO ITS SENSES!

HOLY FATHER— COME ON DOWN!

THANKS JOHNNY! HEY PEOPLE: GIMME A "P"!

P!!

GIMME AN "O"!

O!

GIMME AN "E"!

E!

GIMME A "P"!

P!!

WHASSAT SPELL??

ER...? ??

IT SPELLS "POPE"! ...I SAY IT SPELLS POPE IT SPELLS "POPE"!! ...NOW: WHASSAT SPELL?

HEY JOHNNY — I'M THROWIN' A FANCY DRESS PARTY....

...FOR EVERYONE 'OO OPPOSES WEEMIN PRIESTS!

I'M GONNA WEAR A ZOOT SUIT! — WHAT YOU GONNA WEAR, JOHNNY??

I'M GOING TO PAINT MY FACE RED, FILL MY MOUTH WITH CUSTARD AND GO AS A BOIL!!

69

HEIGH HO! A WINDY DAY!

SKRAUNCH

NYAARRGH!

GOODNESS! A TREE'S JUST FALLEN ON TOP OF ME!

© Steve Bell 1994

NOW—WHERE'S MY COPY OF THE PEDESTRIAN'S CHARTER?!

...AHH....HERE WE ARE: PEDESTRIAN'S CHARTER CHAPTER 15 VERSE 3: "IF YOU ARE INVOLVED IN AN ACCIDENT WITH A TREE......"

22·3·3413

"...YOU ARE FULLY EMPOWERED TO WRITE A LETTER TO THE RELEVANT GOVERN-MENT DEPARTMENT."

© Steve Bell 1994

" THE GOVERNMENT DEPARTMENT IS OBLIGED TO READ YOUR LETTER, AND, IF RESOURCES PERMIT, TO REPLY TO IT."

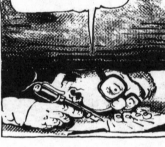

RIGHTO! NOW, WOULD THAT BE MIN.AG.FISH OR D.o.E ??? I'D BETTER SEND ONE TO BOTH......

HERE BIRDIE—I WANT YOU TO RUSH THIS COMPLAINT TO THE MINISTRY OF AGRICULTURE FISH-ERIES AND FOOD....

23·3·3414

...AND THIS OTHER ONE TO THE DEPARTMENT OF THE ENVIRONMENT. GOD SPEED!

PTUI

HEIGH HO! HERE I AM, BEATEN INTO THE GROUND BY A STIFF DOSE OF KNOTTY PINE!

© Steve Bell 1994

...HMMM...I'M ODDLY PUT IN MIND OF MY SCHOOL CAREER....

KNOTTY PINE..........AAAH!...IT BRINGS BACK SUCH MEMORIES OF CHILDHOOD....

24·3·3415

AAAAAHHH!!............WOODWORK!! I FOUND THAT MOST AGREEABLE!

WHAT'S THIS MAJOR MINOR?

© Steve Bell 94

IT'S AN OCCASIONAL TABLE, SIR!

IT'S A PLANK ISN'T IT?

NO, NO; IT'S A SORT OF TABLE YOU USE VERY OCCASIONALLY.... YOU'RE SOMETHING OF A PLANK YOURSELF AREN'T YOU, MAJOR MINOR?

April – May 1994

SMUT SHAG + BEAVER

THE WHOLESOME THREESOME

4·4·3424—

OOYAH!!!

CHRIST ONA BIKE! I'VE DONE ME BITERS IN!!

WHAT ARE THEY PUTTING IN TELEGRAPH POLES THESE DAYS??

THAT'S A REINFORCED CONCRETE BUS STOP BEAVER!

OOOHH... ...URRRGH... I BLAME THE MEDIA!

© Steve Bell 1994

SMUT SHAG + BEAVER

THE WHOLESOME THREESOME

5·4·3425 —

UURRRGHH! ME BITERS!! OOOOHH!

SHADDAP!

HEY! LOOK WHAT I'VE GOT!

NNNGH

WHAT'S THAT?

IT'S A VIDEO

WHAT'S IT FOR?

I BLAME THE MEDIA!

© Steve Bell 1994

SMUT SHAG + BEAVER

THE WHOLESOME THREESOME

-6·4·3426-

UURRRGGH! OOOOOHHH!! AAAAAAARRGGH!

© Steve Bell 1994

MY TOOTHACHE'S BEEN WORSE EVER SINCE WE GOT THAT VIDEO!

SOUNDS LIKE YOU NEED SOMEONE TO WAGGLE A DRILL AROUND INSIDE YOUR SKULL!

VOTE FOR SIGNOR BERLUSCONI!! NOW WHY ON EARTH DID I SAY THAT??

FARZA ITALIA!

-7·4·3427-

HEY! YOU WANNA BE POPULAR?? LISTEN TO ME!..... PSSSPZSSPSSS...

LIGA

HEY! YOU WANT PEOPLE TO TAKE YOU SERIOUSLY? LISTEN TO ME!.... PSSSPZSSSPSS....

OKAY!! WHAT DO WE DO NOW??

© Steve Bell '94

THAT SIGNOR BERLUSCONI HAS MADE QUITE AN IMPACT...

...AND ALL THROUGH SETTING UP A NEW PATRIOTIC MOVEMENT WITH A FOOTBALL CHANT AS ITS TITLE....

HMMMM

© Steve Bell 1994

ENGURLAND

USELESS ENGURLAND

NNNNGH! NNNNGH!!

SPROAT's GUIDE TO MANLY SPORT

14.4.3432

Brian says: "Play with my balls!"

"Please Smut! Please Shag! Please Beaver! Please play!"

© Steve Bell 1994

Ian says: "Come on Smut! Come on Shag! Come on Beaver!"

"Play with Brian's Balls or I'll beat you with this stick!"

SPROAT's GUIDE TO MANLY SPORT

15.4.3433

Ian says "Play Ball!" See Smut run. See Shag run. See Beaver run.

See Smut score. See Shag jump for joy. See Beaver jump for joy.

See Smut jump for Beaver.

© Steve Bell '94

See Smut and Beaver play tonsil hockey.

SPROAT's GUIDE TO MANLY SPORT

16.4.3434

"Bad dog Smut. Bad Beaver." says Ian.

"You must not play tonsil hockey."

"Tonsil hockey is **not** compulsory"

"No drugs for you."

~ Steve Bell 1994 ~

- 25·4·3436 ~

MISTER SHIFTY ☆ PUBLIC RELATIONS

MISTER SHIFTY WILL SEE YOU NOW, MISTER MAJOR.

☆ PUBLIC RELATIONS

© Steve Bell 1994

THANKYOU DAWN. MISTER MAJOR — YOU WANT TO IMPROVE YOUR IMAGE, YOU'VE COME TO THE RIGHT PLACE!

SHIFTY THE SHITHOUSE RAT

REALLY JOHN, IF WE'RE TO MAKE ANY IMPROVEMENT, WE MUST CONSIDER YOUR IMAGE IN THE ROUND....

26·4·3437 -

© Steve Bell '94

...YOUR HAIR'S ALRIGHT AND YOU'VE GOT A LOVELY SMILE........ ...BUT I THINK THERE'S SOMETHING ELSE WE CAN BRING OUT......

THERE YOU ARE! NOW IF YOU'D JUST LEAVE A CHEQUE FOR 62½ GRAND WITH MY ASSISTANT ON YOUR WAY OUT OF THE BUILDING.......

KICK ME VERY HARD

SHIFTY THE SHIT-HOUSE RAT

MISTER SHIFTY ☆ PUBLIC RELATIONS

MISTER SHIFTY! YOU'VE GOT TO HELP ME!

SHIFTY THE SHIT HOUSE RAT

-27·4·3438-

SINCE WE LAST SPOKE MY BOTTOM'S BLACK AND BLUE FROM PEOPLE WHO KEEP COMING UP TO ME IN THE STREET AND KICKING ME.....

KICK ME VERY HARD

...TOTALLY UNPROVOKED! WHAT DO YOU SUGGEST?

- © Steve Bell 1994 -

HMM....I THINK YOU NEED TO PRESENT A GENERALLY LOWER PROFILE..

'KICK ME VERY VERY HARD

WHAT'S THAT?

- 28·4·3439 -

© Steve Bell 1994

3 A.M.... I FEEL A SUDDEN COLDNESS...

...AND WHAT'S THAT GRUMBLING NOISE?

SHNURRDRRR FRRRDRRRR GRRRRRRR

OH MY GAHD! IT'S THE GHOST OF CHECKERS!!

SHNRRRGRRR G'WAN! KICK ME AGAIN!!

June – July 1994

"CHEESE JOB"?? WHAT THE HELL IS A "CHEESE JOB"?

—18·5·3456—

IT'S TOO DISGUSTING TO EVEN BEGIN TO DESCRIBE!........ ...THERE MAY BE CHILDREN OR CONS- -ERVATIVE POLITICIANS READING!

LISTEN — I KNOW FOR A **FACT** THAT MICE ONLY LIVE **2** OR **3** YEARS! IF THIS HAPPENED IN 1986 YOU WOULDN'T HAVE BEEN AROUND!

DEEP REBIRTHING THERAPY MADE ME AWARE THAT IT HAPPENED TO ME IN A PREVIOUS EXISTENCE!

NYAAAA!

YOU GOT SOME EXPLAINING TO DO, BUSTER!

©Steve Bell 94

YOU'RE IN SERIOUS TROUBLE, SIR. I'M GOING TO HAVE TO ADMINISTER HALLUCINOGENIC DRUGS TO VERIFY THIS MOUSE'S STORY.

19·5·3457

IS IT TRUE THAT YOU WERE PHYSICALLY MANIPULATED BY THIS CAT IN 1986?

GLORK

©Steve Bell 94

OOEY OOEY OOEY OOEY OOEY OOEY OOEY OOEY OOEY HE PAWED ME!! HE PAWED ME!!

WHAT IS THIS CRAP?

REMEMBER— YOU ARE ON OATH

OOEY OOEY OOEY OOEY HE F***** PAWED ME, THE F****R!!

I'M SERVIN' YOU WITH A SUBPŒNA, SIR!

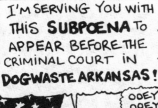

I'M SERVING YOU WITH THIS SUBPOENA TO APPEAR BEFORE THE CRIMINAL COURT IN DOGWASTE ARKANSAS!

OOEY OOEY OOEY

20·5·3458

...TO ANSWER THE CHARGE THAT YOU DID WILFULLY MOLEST THIS MOUSE IN 1986.

OOEY OOEY OOEY OOEY

©Steve Bell 94

OOOEY OOEY OOEY OOOWOW! CHECK OUT THE SIZE o' THAT SUBPOENA! THAT'S ONE OF THE BIGGEST SUBPOENAS I'VE EVER SEEN IN MY LIFE!!

SHADDAP!!

OOEY OOEY OOOEY OOEY OOEY OOEY OOOEY OOEY OOEEEE!

YOU CAN'T DO THIS TO ME, YOU KNOW. I'M NOT JUST ANY CAT....

WHY NOT, SLEAZEBAG?

21·5·3459—

I AM THE MOST POWERFUL CAT ON EARTH!

SO WHAT?

©Steve Bell 1994

·I AM AN INSTITUTION AND AS SUCH SHOULD BE PROTECTED RATHER THAN UNDERMINED!

HE'S RIGHT, MY FRIEND!

SO I WANT YOU TO WANT YOU TO GO OUT AND PROCURE ME A COUPLE OF CUTE LITTLE BROWN MICE!

YESSIR!

23.5.3460 —

WHITE CLIFFS AT TWELVE O'CLOCK, BLUEBIRD LEADER!

WE'RE GOING IN LOW!

YOU'RE GOING IN TOO LOW, BLUEBIRD LEADER!!

STUFF AND NONSENSE! OUR FLIGHT PATH IS THE ONLY POSSIBLE ONE!

© Steve Bell 1994

BLUEBIRD LEADER — ARE YOU O.K??

I HAVE A SLIGHT HEADACHE BUT THE WORLD IS FREE!

BLUEBIRD LEADER

© Steve Bell 1994

GRUNT

PHEW!

TING TING

REACH FOR THE SKY, MADAM — THE WORLD IS FREE!

POST OFFICE

— 24.5.3461 —

BLUEBIRD LEADER

THIS POST OFFICE IS NOW FREE, MA'AM!!...

25.5.3462 —

I'M GOING TO LOCK YOU IN THE BACK ROOM WHILE MICHAEL HERE REMOVES YOUR ASSETS!

Royal Swag

© Steve Bell '96

YOU DON'T LOOK VERY HAPPY, MA'AM, WHY AREN'T YOU HAPPY? YOU SHOULD BE HAPPY! I THINK YOU'VE BEEN GOT AT BY THE MEDIA!!

BE HAPPY! DANCE! COME ON! FREE UP!! JOY! JOY!!

BLAM BLAM

CLEAR FOR TAKE-OFF, BLUEBIRD LEADER

Royal Swag

— 26.5.3463 —

ROGER, APE LEADER AIR SPEED 30 KNOTS; WIND SPEED 20 KNOTS...

© Steve Bell 1994 —

THROTTLE UP!.... UNDERCARRIAGE UP!

Royal Swag

BOTTOMS UP!

Royal Swag

86

89

RAT TAT TAT

WHAT DO YOU WANT?

LORD ARCHER — WOULD YOU SPARE ME A MOMENT OF YOUR VALUABLE TIME?

WHAT IS IT, DARLING? IT'S A MONKEY TRYING TO SELL WASHING POWDER

DON'T BUY ANYTHING UNTIL I'VE HAD A LOOK AT IT, DARLING!

© Steve Bell 1994

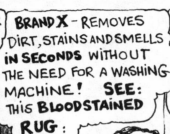

I PROMISE YOU, LORD ARCHER — YOU'LL NEVER REGRET TAKING A LOOK AT THIS PRODUCT!

BRAND X — REMOVES DIRT, STAINS AND SMELLS IN SECONDS WITHOUT THE NEED FOR A WASHING MACHINE! SEE: THIS BLOODSTAINED RUG:

INTO THE HOT! INTO THE COLD! UP TO THE LIGHT — SHINING AND BRIGHT!

THANKS TO HEATHER!

UP TO THE NOSE — SMELLS LIKE A ROSE!! HERE! TRY IT!

I STILL SEE A FLICKER OF DOUBT IN YOUR EYES, LORD ARCHER. THAT'S NOT SURPRISING. PEOPLE JUST CAN'T BELIEVE WHAT BRAND X IS CAPABLE OF!

...SO TO PROVE IT TO YOU I'M GOING TO GIVE BRAND X THE ULTIMATE CHALLENGE: A DOCKER'S SOCK MARINADED FOR THREE HOT WEEKS....

...IN A MIXTURE OF RANCID HADDOCK AND A DOG'S LOOSE STOOLS........ INTO THE HOT! INTO THE COLD! UP TO THE LIGHT — SHINING AND BRIGHT!...

...UP TO THE NOSE....

GOOD GRIEF! MARY!! IT SMELLS LIKE A ROSE!!!

© Steve Bell 1994

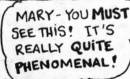

MARY — YOU MUST SEE THIS! IT'S REALLY QUITE PHENOMENAL!

THIS MONKEY TOOK ONE OF THE FILTHIEST, SMELLIEST SOCKS YOU'VE EVER SEEN, DIPPED IT IN A SOLUTION OF THIS STUFF....

...AND IT CAME PERFECTLY CLEAN IN A MATTER OF SECONDS! QUICK!! GET THE DIRTY WASHING BASKET! I WANT TO TRY IT OUT!

WE DON'T HAVE A DIRTY WASHING BASKET, JEFFREY

© Steve Bell 1994

August – September 1994

95

96

-25·7·3496-

PZAM

MAM-MON...

HOW I LOVE YA HOW I LOVE YA MA DEAR OL' MAMMON...

© Steve Bell 1994

GABE! HOW'S THE BOOKDEAL LOOKING?

-26·7·3497-

VERY WELL, G....

SCHMOOZ SCHMOOZ

© Steve Bell '94

...RUPERT IS WAVING A REALLY ENORMOUS CHEQUE UNDER MY NOSE EVEN AS WE SPEAK.....

BANK OF MURDOCHIA
$1,000,000,000,000,000,000,000,000,000,000,000

...HE'S PREPARED TO GO TO ALMOST INFINITE LENGTHS TO AQUIRE A TEARAWAY BIBLE, VOLUME THREE WITH A LOT OF TIT! WHAT D'YOU THINK?

....BARP!

MYSELF ALMIGHTY! IF RUPERT WANTS TIT IN VOLUME THREE, RUPERT CAN HAVE AS MUCH AS HE WANTS!

23·7·3498-

...REMEMBER - YOU'RE GHOSTING THIS, SO IT'S DOWN TO YOU, GABE!

BLORK

I WANT THE CENTRAL CHARACTER TO BE A RADICAL RIGHT WING SHEILA WHO'S PREPARED TO TAKE HER SHIRT OFF...

GARP!

© Steve Bell

...AND I WANT YOU TO GIVE THE WHOLE STORY A EURO-SCEPTICAL SLANT....

THASSH VISIONARY RUPE!

CRIPES LARRY! YOU LOOK HOT!

28·7·3499-

STRIKE A LIGHT!

PZAM

SHEILA — I AM THE ARCHANGEL GABRIEL AND YOU'RE GOING TO HAVE A BABY!

YOU'RE ROUND THE FLAMIN' TWIST!

© Steve Bell 1994

97

YES! YOU, SHEILA ARE GOING TO HAVE A BABY!!

29·7·3500

YOU'RE CRAZY! THE NEAREST MAN'S FOUR HUNDRED MILES AWAY IN ALICE SPRINGS!

...AND I WOULDN'T TOUCH YOU WITH A FLAMIN' BARGEPOLE!

YOU DON'T UNDERSTAND: GOD WANTS YOU TO HAVE HIS BABY!

GOD CAN GO AND BITE HIS BUM!

©Steve Bell 1994

30·7·3501

PZAM

LISTEN SHEILA — GOD HAS AUTHORISED ME TO OFFER YOU THIS CHEQUE FOR $250,000....

©Steve Bell 1994

...IN RETURN FOR HAVING HIS BABY. WHAT DO YOU SAY?

I SAY GOD CAN AFFORD IT. MAKE IT $50 MILLION AND WE'VE GOT A DEAL!

THAT'S JUST FOR HAVING IT — IF HE WANTS IT BROUGHT UP IT'LL COST EXTRA TELEPHONE NUMBERS!

1·8·3502

HMMM.... ...MMM....

WHAT DO YOU THINK OF IT SO FAR, G?

©Steve Bell 1994—

NOT BAD, GABE — I LIKE THE IDEA OF SETTING THE BIBLE VOLUME THREE IN AUSTRALIA....

DO YOU G?

I LIKE THE BAD LANGUAGE: "BITE YOUR BUM!" THAT GAVE ME A GOOD CHUCKLE!!

THANK YOU, G! EXCUSE ME WHILE I TAKE THIS CALL

BREEEP BREEP

GABRIEL — I GOT YOUR FAX. I MUST MAKE CLEAR I WILL NOT HAVE TOILET TALK IN ANY OF MY PUBLICATIONS!

VOLUME THREE

...AND I TELL YOU THIS....

2·8·3503

...IT'S ALL MUMBO JUMBO....

...BUT REMEMBER: IT'S THE BEST SORT OF MUMBO JUMBO!

IT'S PURE......

...BOLLOCKS, AND WHAT'S MORE: I NEED THE MONEY!

—©Steve Bell '94—

BAH!

WHAT'S HAPPENING TO STANDARDS DOWN THERE?

IF YOU DON'T LIKE THE MUMBO JUMBO, GET OUT OF THE BONEYARD!!

RESIGN!

RESIGN!

..SO YOU SEE: THERE IS NOTHING "OUT THERE"...

"GOD" IS AN IDEA.... ...THINK ABOUT IT!...

GOD IS A LIGHTBULB..... ....A LARGE BONE.... ...A PAIR OF KNOCKERS... ...A GIGANTIC BOOT...... ...OOER!! MORNING BISHOP!!

GULP

HONEST....I WAS ONLY DOING WHAT THEY TAUGHT ME IN VICAR SCHOOL, BISHOP......

SAY THE FIRST THING THAT COMES INTO YOUR HEAD THEN RAMBLE ON FOR FIFTEEN MINUTES...

IT'S A SURE FIRE TECHNIQUE! YOU EVER HEAR 'THOUGHT FOR THE DAY'??

IT'S ALL BOLLOCKS, BUT IT'S BETTER THAN AN EMBARRASSING SILENCE!

YOU WANNA WASH YOUR MOUTH OUT!!

I'M GONNA WASH YOUR MOUTH OUT....

...THEN I'M PUTTIN' YOU ON THE FREE TRANSFER LIST!!

ER...BISHOP!.... CAN I STILL WEAR MY COLLAR BACK TO FRONT?

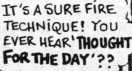

AMEX TREESLAYER GOLD — ANYTHING ELSE JUST WON'T....

...TAKE THE HEADS OFF POUNCING JAGUARS.....

...COOL ME DOWN WHEN THE JUNGLE GETS HOT......

...FIT NEATLY BETWEEN MY BUTTOCKS WHEN I'M FAST ASLEEP...

GOOD LORD! THIS GUNGE ON THE LINO!.....

...IT'S ONE OF THE PUREST FORMS OF LARD KNOWN TO MANKIND!!

TELL ME — FROM WHENCE DOES THIS COME? WHERE DO YOU GATHER THIS SUPERB LARD?

IF YOU CAN OBTAIN ME REGULAR SUPPLIES OF THIS FABULOUS LARD.....

...I WILL SUPPLY YOU WITH ALL THE BANANAS AND PEANUTS YOU COULD EVER POSSIBLY WANT!!.....

....THERE'S ONLY ONE CONDITION: YOU MUST STOP BREEDING NOW!!

WHEN YOU'VE QUITE FINISHED YOUR FEAST OF BANANAS IN LARD....

I SHALL EXPLAIN A SIMPLE AND EFFECTIVE AND EARTH FRIENDLY METHOD OF CONTRACEPTION

I WANT YOU TO SET ABOUT EACH OTHER'S SENSITIVE PARTS WITH COPIES OF THIS MAGAZINE

COR....I WAS REALLY IN THE MOOD, AND NOW....WELL....

September – October 1994

I TELL YOU IT WASN'T MY FAULT, FATHER—IT WAS A DAMNED PAPPARAZZI WITH AN UNFAIRLY LONG LENS!

PULL!

IDIOT BOY—THE TWO GOLDEN RULES OF ROYALTY ARE: WE DON'T GO TO THE TOILET, AND WE NEVER TAKE OUR KIT OFF!!

BLAM

BLAM

OH COME OFF IT, PA!!

GET REAL!

IS IT LOADED, GRAHAM?

AFTER CENTURIES OF BEING BLOWN OUT OF THE SKY....

...AT LAST WE SHALL BE AVENGED... ...AAAAHH!

KRON PRINZ CHARLES NACKT IN DAS SCHEISS-HAUS

I TELL YA, SOCKS: THIS HAITI THING— (a): IT'S ABOUT HUMAN RIGHTS;

YOU MEAN THE RIGHT TO KEEP THE BLACKS OUT??

YEAH, WELL: (b): IT'S ABOUT RESTORING DEMOCRACY AND (c): IT'S ABOUT PRESERVING U.S. CREDIBILITY....

DO YOU INTEND TO KEEP THE TROOPS IN THERE PERMANENTLY??

YEAH, WELL, ER.... ...NO...

THAT TAKES CARE OF (b) AND (c)— YOU'VE GOT TO FACE IT BILL...

FACE WHAT?

IT'S ABOUT FISH! YOU'VE GOTTA GO IN BECAUSE THERE'S A LOT OF OUR FISH ROUND THERE!!

TELL THE PEOPLE THE TRUTH, BILL!! HAITI IS ABOUT FISH! FISH! FISH!

WO... SOCKS! EASY!!

THE PUBLIC WON'T SWALLOW IT IF I SAY I'M INVADING HAITI BECAUSE OF THE FISH!

BULLSHIT, BILL!!

THE PUBLIC LOVE TO SWALLOW FISH!! BE HONEST! BE STRAIGHT!! IT'S BETTER IN THE LONG RUN....BUT YOU GOTTA DROP SOME FREE RADIOS ON LITTLE ROCK TO TELL 'EM WHAT'S WHAT!!

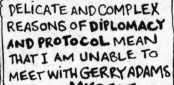

SOCKS—I NEED YOUR HELP!

26·9·3532

DELICATE AND COMPLEX REASONS OF DIPLOMACY AND PROTOCOL MEAN THAT I AM UNABLE TO MEET WITH GERRY ADAMS MYSELF...

HRRMMPH

...SO I WANT YOU AND TEDDY TO TAKE HIM OUT AND SHOW HIM A GOOD TIME.

ONLY IF I CAN TAKE HIM OUT ON THE TILES!

— © Steve Bell 1994 ·

A NATION ONSHE AGAIN!! HAVE 'NOTHER BIG ONE GERRY!

I DON'T DRINK

PADDY

—27·9·3533—

HERE—HAVE A SMOKE! YOU WANNA SPLIFF? A LI'L TOOT, MAYBE?

I DON'T SMOKE AND I DON'T DO DROGS

SOUNDS LIKE YOU'RE READY TO CLIMB UP ON THE ROOF WITH ME AND SING, GERRY!

SHEEEE!

WELL I CAN NEITHER SING NOR CLIMB, BUT I CAN DANCE A LITTLE!

HOLY SHIT! WHAT'RE WE DOIN' UP HERE?

C'MON GERRY—SHOW US WHAT YOU CAN DO!

28·9·3534

I'LL JUST SIT HERE AND SCREAM QUIETLY WHILE YOU DO YOUR ETHNIC DANCE ROUTINE

AAAAAAHH...

— © Steve Bell '94 —

...A HIPPETY HIPPETY HIPPETY HIPPETY HIPPETY HIPPETY HIP...

AÏEEEE YOWW YOWW YOWW!

...A HIPPETY HIPPETY HIPPETY HIPPETY...

HEY GERRY! YOU WANT A WOMAN AND A CAR FOR LATER ON?

ANY O' YOU GUYS WANNA LIFT HOME? AAAAAARRGHH!!!

HEY! TEDDY'S FALLEN OFF THE ROOF!

NYAA-HIPPETY HIPPETY HIPPETY HIPPETY....

KRASH

—29·9·3535—

I LOVE THE ROUTINE, GERRY—I GIVE YOU TOP MARKS FOR LEGWORK!

...HIPPETY HIPPETY....

I OBJECT!

I DEMAND THAT I BE ALLOWED TO PUT THE BRITISH POINT OF VIEW HERE AND NOW!!

HIPPETY HIP....

© Steve Bell '94

108

110

LET'S GET SERIOUS, JOHN — SINGED AER-TEX DOES NOT SUIT YOUR COMPLEXION!

COLOUR ME BOLLOX image consultants

CRISP PINK IS A BIG IMPROVEMENT, BUT GET A HAIRSTYLE, GET SOME TEETH!

YOU'RE FEELING MORE CONFIDENT ALREADY — I CAN TELL, JOHN!

14.10.3547

MMMM — WE'RE GETTING SOMEWHERE, BUT THERE'S STILL ONE THING....

...HAVE YOU EVER THOUGHT OF PUTTING YOUR HEAD WHERE YOUR BOTTOM IS AND WALKING AROUND ON YOUR HANDS?

COLOUR ME BOLLOX image consultant

SHAKE

IT MAY TAKE SOME DOING, BUT IT COULD BE WELL WORTH IT....

IT'S EARLY DAYS, BUT I THINK WE MAY BE ON A WINNER!

15.10.3548

WAKEY WAKEY RISE AND SHI-INE!

TIME FOR YOUR MORNING FLAP!!

COME ON NOW! DON'T BE SHY!

SORRY DOLL — I DON'T GET OUT O' BED FOR LESS THAN A MONKEY THESE DAYS!

©Steve Bell 1994

HERE'S YOUR MONKEY! FIVE HUNDRED LOVELY SMACKERS!

JUST LAY IT ON THE BOTTOM O' THE CAGE, DOLL....

COME ON CHEEKY! WHO'S A PRETTY BOY THEN?

YOU ASKIN' ME A QUESTION? THAT'LL BE ANOTHER ONE AND A HALF GRAND, DOLL

25.10.3550

— ©Steve Bell 1994

November – December 1994

COME ON! CO-OME ON! WHO'S A PRETTY BOY? WHO HASN'T HAD HIS BREAKFAST THEN?

WHO'S A GRUMPY BOY? THREE QUESTIONS — THAT'LL COST YOU FOUR AND A HALF LONG ONES, DOLL!

© Steve Bell '94

HERE YOU ARE THEN — FOUR AND A HALF THOUSAND LOVELY SMACKERS! JUST LAY 'EM ON THE BOTTOM OF THE CAGE, DOLL

...NOW GET LOST — I GOTTA CALL A MAN ABOUT A DOG!

HELLO CHEEKY! DID YOU MISS ME? JUST PUT FIFTEEN HUNDRED QUID ON THE FLOOR OF THE CAGE, DOLL!

- 27·10·3552 -

YOU LAVISH FAR TOO MUCH ON THAT BIRD, MAVIS! BELIEVE ME DORA — HE'S WORTH EVERY PENNY, AREN'T YOU CHEEKY?

© Steve Bell '94

THAT'S BROUGHT IT UP TO THREE LONG ONES.... I TELL YOU THIS — WHEN HE SOUNDS OFF HE'S WORTH HIS WEIGHT IN GOLD: LISTEN —

I'M WORRIED ABOUT ALL THIS COLOURED IMMIGRATION! IT'S TIME WE TOOK A STAND!! OOO·OOO! OOO·OOO!

THEY COME HERE, ALL SHAPES SIZES AND COLOURS, THEY HANG AROUND ON OUR TELEGRAPH POLES, THEY EAT OUR FLIES,...

- 28·10·3553 -

THEY SHIT ALL OVER OUR STATUES, IT'S DRIVING ME.....

...OFF ME PERCH! ROUND THE BEND! WE MUST ACT!!

STONE ME! THE OLD BAGS HAVE FAINTED!

WHIMPER! SQUEAK!

© Steve Bell 1994

SHOP AT HARRODS! STAY AT THE RITZ!!! TINY ROWLAND IS A SHITBAG!

- 29·10·3554 -

DORA! WAKE UP!! YOUR PARROT!!!

HE'S BEEN SEEING SOMEONE ELSE!! I BUY MY MONKEYS FROM HARRODS FOOD HALL!

© Steve Bell '94

CHEEKY!! HOW COULD YOU?? YOU INFERRING I'M NOT STRAIGHT AS A DIE? YOU WANT A WORD WITH MY LAWYER?

115

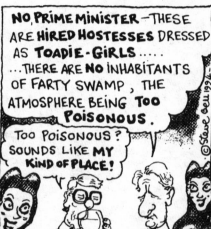

SEEMS **I'VE** GOT THE **MIDAS** TOUCH, EH SIR ROBIN??

...I MEAN IT'S NOT EVERYONE CAN INSPIRE AN ENORMOUSLY WEALTHY PERSON TO MAKE **SIXTY MILLION QUID** IN AN **AFTERNOON**....

...OUT OF A **FARTY OLD SWAMP**!

J'ACCUSE!

OH MY **GOD**!! THERE'S A **MOLE** IN MY **UNDERPANTS**!!

GO **FARTYSWAMP** plc

SIR ROBIN!! I WUNT YOU TO **INVESTIGATE** THESE DRINKS!

WHERE DID THEY COME FROM?? **WHO** GAVE THEM TO ME??

GO **FARTYSWAMP**

SNIFF

IT'S **GIN**, PRIME MINISTER, WITH SOME **TONIC** ADDED. IT CAME FROM A **BOTTLE** WHICH I BELIEVE CAME FROM A **FACTORY**. I'M SATISFIED THAT THE **CHAIRMAN OF FARTY SWAMP INTERNATIONAL**

...HAD ABSOLUTELY **NOTHING WHATSOEVER** TO DO WITH THE MANUFACTURE OF **THIS DRINK**!

SO THERE! NYAA NYARDY NYAA NYAAA!!

THE **BALLAD** OF *Sleazy Rider*

THOG THOG THOG

THE RITZ

SKREEEE

Sleazy Rider

TWO MEN IN SEARCH OF **FREEBONIA**...

THE RITZ

THOG THOG

THAT'S **ROOM SERVICE**! YOU KNOW WHAT **ROOM SERVICE** IS, DON'T YOU BIG BOY?

SURE

ROOM SERVICE? SEND ME UP A **CHICK** AND A PACK OF **BUTTER**....

...I CAN'T GET MY **HELMET** OFF....

117

119

I HAVE A DREAM, MR HURD.... A GIANT **EXPLODING DAM** CREATING AN ENVIRONMENT...

FARTYSWAMP INTERNATIONAL EXPLODING DAM

...IDEAL FOR **HUNTING NEWTS**. THEN, WITH TRIED AND TESTED **BRITISH ANTI-NEWT TECHNOLOGY**, WHICH I TRUST **YOU** WILL SUPPLY, MR HURD,.....

...WE GO FORWARD TO THE FOUNDING OF A **NEW WORLD ORDER!**

DRONE DRONE

RADICAL! STIMULATING!

AïEEE! AïEEE!

I CAN STATE QUITE CATEGORICALLY THAT THERE IS **NO PRECISE CAUSAL LINK**.....

...BETWEEN OUR BRIBING AND **SELLING OFFENSIVE TECHNOLOGY** TO CERTAIN **REGIMES**...

...AND THE REPORTED **DEATHS** OF LARGE NUMBERS OF **SUBJECTS** OF THOSE **REGIMES**......

NO, THE FACT OF THE MATTER IS: **BENT WOGS** ARE PLOTTING TO UNDERMINE OUR NATIONAL INTEGRITY!

I'VE GOT YOU WHERE I WANT YOU NOW, YOU **EVIL OLD BAT!**

I'M GOING TO SUBMERGE YOU IN A BATH OF **MOLTEN BRASS!**

...AND YOU'LL NEVER BOTHER ME AGAIN!!

OH SHIT! SHE'S STILL ALIVE!!

MORE! MORE BRASS!

OH **GOD!** WHAT HAVE I **DONE?**

I AM THE **BRASS BEAST!!**

PING PING

A HORSE! A HORSE! FETCH ME A **HORSE!**

CLANK CLANG

I RIDE TO ARMS PURSUIVANT DEXTER GULES!.....

SORRY MA'AM - I DON'T KNOW ANY HORSE

FETCH ME A **SEALION** THEN! - IF I CANNOT RIDE I MUST **BARK!**

 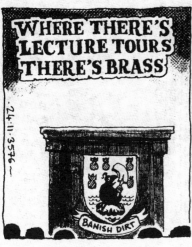  

January – March 1995

125

TONY BLAIR'S SCHOOLDAYS

7·12·3587

REVEREND MOTHER— I'VE JUST DISCOVERED SOMETHING QUITE DREADFUL!

WHAT IS IT MY SON?

I'M NOT A CATHOLIC!

HEAVENS ABOVE!

THIS IS SERIOUS, YOUNG BLAIR! I FEAR WE MAY BE OBLIGED TO LET YOU GO!

...BUT FIRST: REMIND ME HOW MUCH YOUR FATHER EARNS.....?

HALLELUJAH! I'M SAVED! THANK GOD FOR SELECTION!

TONY BLAIR'S SCHOOLDAYS

8·12·3588

THE YEARS PASS

YOU'VE BECOME SOMETHING OF A REBEL, YOUNG BLAIR.

YOU'VE BEEN USING BAD LANGUAGE! DON'T TRY AND DENY IT!!

WHO TOLD YOU THAT, REV'D MOTHER?

NEVER MIND WHO TOLD ME, WHY HAVE YOU BEEN UTTERING PROFANITIES?

OK—I ADMIT IT REVEREND MOTHER...

I HAVE USED SWEAR WORDS..... .....BUT I DIDN'T PRONOUNCE THEM PROPERLY!

©Steve Bell '94

TONY BLAIR'S SCHOOLDAYS

9·12·3589

MORE YEARS PASS

SACRED HEART OF THE BLEEDING CHERUB CND BRANCH

ARE WE ALL READY FOR THE BIG MARCH, CHAPS?

YAY TONY!

YOU LEAD, WE'LL FOLLOW TONY!

A-ONE- TWO-THREE -FOUR.....

BAN THE BOMB FOR EVERMORE— OR UNTIL IT INTERFERES WITH OUR CAREERS

©Steve Bell 1994

TONY BLAIR'S SCHOOL-DAYS

10·12·3590

TIME FOR SOME HEAVY PROGRESSIVE MUSIC, CATS

©Steve Bell 1994

JUH-JUH-JUH- JESUS JUH-JUH- -JESUS JUH-JUH- -JESUS —

JUH-JUH- -JESUS JUH-JUH- JESUS WAH-WAH-

—WANTS ME FOR A SUNBEAM!

...DESPITE WHAT YOU MAY HAVE READ IN SOME OF THE NEWSPAPERS...

...IT GIVES ME THE GREATEST PLEASURE TO RETURN ONCE AGAIN TO 'OLDMANK'!...

...AS MY HUSBAND LIKES TO REFER TO YOUR GREAT CITY...

...AS I SAID MYSELF: IF YOU THINK MANCHESTER IS A DUMP, YOU OUGHT TO TAKE A LOOK AT SOME OF THOSE RUSSIAN BURGS!

IN'T SHE LUV'LY, CHOOK?

MARVELLOUS SENSE OF HUMOUR!

...OF COURSE I NOW REALISE THAT MY GOING TO MOSCOW...

...AND ACCEPTING THE HOSPITALITY OF THAT FAT RUSSIAN INEBRIATE.....

...WAS A NAÏVE AND STUPID MISTAKE. I THOUGHT IT MIGHT BE BOTH EXHILARATING AND A BIT OF FUN!

HOW WRONG I WAS. THE WORDS "THOROUGHLY ARSED OFF" FAIL TO CONVEY THE EXTENT OF MY DISILLUSIONMENT WITH THE RUSSIAN CAP-ITALIST SYSTEM!

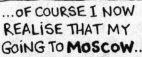

...YOU MAY HAVE HEARD THE WORDS "SCANDINAVIAN MODEL" BANDIED ARINED IN THE MEDIA OF LATE....

I MUST CONFESS MY HEART SANK AT THE PROSPECT OF A WHOLE NEW SET OF HEADLINES:

'CHARLES CAUGHT IN FLAGRANTE WITH SWEDISH MEATBALL'; 'VIKING BIRD BARED ALL IN BID TO BEAR CROWN'...

...ETCETERA, ETCETERA... ...VAIR FUNNY I DON'T THINK!

EY-OOP! DRIZZLE'S BACK!

YOUR MAJESTY— —I HAVE A PROPOSITION I WISH TO MAKE TO YOU.....SSSSLLLP?

AND WHAT WOULD THAT BE, PRIME MINISTER?

I'D LIKE YOU TO STAND FOR THE CONSERVATIVE PARTY THE NEXT TIME WE HAVE A BY-ELECTION!

WHAT WOULD BE IN IT FOR ME, JOHN? SSSSSLLLPP...

127

WHAT'S THE BOOK, BILL?

THE THREEFOLD PATH TO AFFIRMATIVE POPULAR INTERFACE BY CHARLES FORKHEAD III

IT'S DYNAMITE SOCKS! —IT'S KIND OF A NEW AGE THING—!

THREEFOLD PATH?

CHARLES FORKHEAD III

WHAT DOES THE THREEFOLD PATH INVOLVE?

ONE: CHOOSE VALUES; TWO: VALUE CHOICE; THREE: HAVE SEX WITH BABOONS

"CHOOSE VALUES" AND "VALUE CHOICE" —THAT SOUNDS LIKE STANDARD NEW AGE HORSE SHIT....

THE THREEFOLD PATH TO AFFIRMATIVE POPULAR INTERFACE BY CHARLES FORKHEAD III

...BUT WHY "HAVE SEX WITH BABOONS"?? I DON'T GET IT!

YOU DON'T WANT TO GET HUNG UP ON THE "WHY" THING, SOCKS

WE'VE GOT TO "THINK WIN"! WE'VE GOT TO BE PRO-ACTIVE OTHERWISE THE BABOONS MIGHT RUN AWAY

SOCKS—I'D LIKE YOU TO MEET NEW AGE GURU, CHARLES FORKHEAD III

IT FEELS POSITIVE TO INTERFACE WITH YOU, LITTLE FURRY BUDDY! LET'S FOCUS!

LET'S HOLD HANDS, LET'S CROSS OUR EYES, LET'S THINK ABOUT THOSE LITTLE PURPLE ASSES!

SOUNDS WORSE THAN EVER, BILL

SPUAWK

BEEP

HEY! I SEE WHAT YOU'RE DOING WRONG!

YOU HAVE TO BLOW THE SAX AND INHALE THE JOINT!

SQUEEE

MMMP

?

SHADDAP!

HEY! THERE'S THE **ELEPHANT**! LET'S **FOCUS** ON THE ELEPHANT!

HE'S TURNED AWAY! WE'LL HAVE TO FOCUS ON HIS **FLIPSIDE**!

I'VE GOT IT! YES! I CAN SEE IT!!

I CAN SEE **NEWT** IN **3D** COMING OUT OF THE ELEPHANT'S ASS!

I GOT IT! I GOT IT!

SPEAK NEWT! WE'RE **FOCUSSED**!

YOU, CLINTON, ARE A **SICK**, **EVIL**, **SEXUALLY PERVERTED** SPEND-O-CRAT!!

I'M GONNA **CLEAN** YOU UP REAL GOOD!

THAT'S A FUNNY THING FOR AN **ELEPHANT'S ASS** TO SAY!

IT'S GIVING ME A **HEADACHE**!

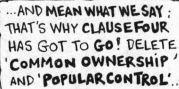

WE MUST **SAY** WHAT WE **MEAN**...

...AND **MEAN** WHAT WE **SAY**; THAT'S WHY **CLAUSE FOUR** HAS GOT TO **GO**! DELETE '**COMMON OWNERSHIP**' AND '**POPULAR CONTROL**'...

...AND INSERT "**DO AS TONY SAYS OR HE'LL SCREAM AND SCREAM.**"

WHAT HAVE WE GOT? A **RADICAL AGENDA**!

WHAT DOES THAT **MEAN**??

WHATEVER YOU SAY!

O.K. — LET'S ADDRESS THE **ISSUES**!

THANKS TO HEATHER

THE PANTS! HE'S WEARING THE **PANTS** OF POWER!

SIR – ARE YOU INTERESTED IN LABOUR'S **RADICAL AGENDA**?

WHAT'S THAT THEN?

WELL, '**AGENDA**' MEANS A SORT OF **LIST** OF WHAT YOU DO IN A **COMMITTEE**...

...AND '**RADICAL**' IS TO DO WITH **ROOTS**, BASED ON THE LATIN WORD FOR '**RADISH**'....

© Steve Bell 1995

**** OFF!

© Steve Bell 1995

...THERE'S NO MISTAKING WHO **WEARS THE PANTS** IN **THIS PARTY**!!

HE WHO WIELDS THE **PANTS OF POWER** SHALL **INHERIT THE EARTH**!!

HEY! MAYBE THAT'S EXACTLY THE **SET OF WORDS** WE NEED TO REPLACE **CLAUSE FOUR**!

THANKS TO HEATHER

WHAT WAS THAT AGAIN? "**HE OR SHE WHO WIELDS**...

HE SHE OR **NON-SEXED** COLLEAGUE!

..OK – "**HE, SHE OR NON-SEXED** WHO WIELDS THE **PANTS OF POWER**...

CLAUSE IV REPLACEMENT DEBATE

"...**SHALL INHERIT THE EARTH**."

MMM.... IT'S A BIT **STARK**

AND IT DOESN'T MENTION **QUALITY**, **CHOICE** OR **OPPORTUNITY**

20·1·3613

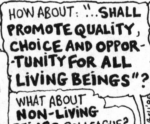
HOW ABOUT: "...**SHALL PROMOTE QUALITY, CHOICE AND OPPORTUNITY FOR ALL LIVING BEINGS**"?

WHAT ABOUT **NON-LIVING BEINGS**, COLLEAGUE?

© Steve Bell '95

O.K. "HE, SHE OR **NON-SEXED** WHO WIELDS THE **PANTS OF POWER** SHALL **PROMOTE QUALITY, CHOICE AND OPPORTUNITY FOR ALL LIVING AND NON-LIVING BEINGS**"

COLLEAGUES – WE ARE **CONFIDENT** IN OUR **CORE VALUES**...

SPEAK, YOUR **NEWNESS**!

...WE VALUE THE **PANTS OF POWER**!

YOU CAN **DO NO WRONG**, **PANT WIELDER**!

..BECAUSE **PERPETUAL MODERNISATION** PLUS **POWER PANTS** MEANS.......

© Steve Bell '95

I CAN FLY ♪ I CAN FLY ♪ I CAN FLY !!!

138

143

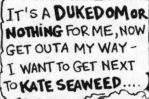

WHAT DO YOU MEAN YOU **HAVEN'T GOT A** QUARTER MILLION QUID?

LIFFEN - CAN'T YOU DO IT ON THE **NHF**?

NHF? NHS?

N.H.S?!! ARFARFARF ARF!!

WHAT'S NHS? IS IT ONE O' THEM **NEW WONDER DRUGS**?

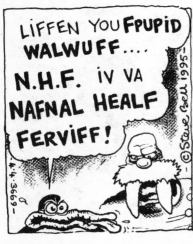

LIFFEN YOU **FPUPID WALWUFF**.... N.H.F. iV VA **NAFNAL HEALF FERVIFF**!

CAN'T YOU **FiFF MY PEEFF** ORRA NAFNAL HEALF?

OH **THAT**!? YOU MEAN THE **NATIONAL HEALTH SERVICE**?

COURSE I CAN! I CAN FIX YOUR TEETH ON THE **NATIONAL HEALTH SERVICE**!

...OR I CAN DO YOU A **PROPER JOB** — KNOW WHAT I MEAN?

NUDGE

ARE YOU PELLIN' ME I WON' GEWWA PWOPER **JOB** ORRA **NAFNAL HEALF FERVIFF??**

NUDGE

NO, NO - OF COURSE YOU GET A **PROPER JOB** ON THE NATIONAL HEALTH!

WINK WINK

NUDGE

BUT IF YOU **GO PRIVATE** THERE ARE CERTAIN 'REFINEMENTS' OR 'OPPORTUNITIES FOR CHOICE' THAT YOU GET.....

INNAT CAFE, GIMME A NHF JOB!

CAN I HAVE THE **FUNNY PINK MOUTHWASH** NOW?

NO

GOOD LORD!

?

LOOK AT THAT POOR BASTARD WITH THE **NHS TEETH**!

TRY AND **ACT NATURALLY**... ...WE MUSTN'T EMBARRASS HIM!

HERE JAWS — — HERE'S **50p** TO GO AND BUY YOUR-SELF SOME **THIN GRUEL**

146

- 7·4·3672 -

- 8·4·3673 -

- 10·4·3674 -

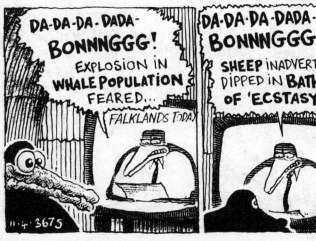

11·4·3675

April – May 1995

I'M TRULY SHOCKED AT THE LEVEL OF EDUCATION ON THESE ISLANDS!

STICK IT UP YOUR CHURCHILL, CHUM!

2·5·3687

THE INSOUCIANT IGNORANCE OF THESE SHEEP TAKES MY BREATH AWAY!

CHURCHILLS TO YOU, MATE—I'VE GOT A DEGREE!

A DEGREE?!? WHAT SORT OF DEGREE??

©Steve Bell 1995

I'VE GOT A B.A.A.A.A.AA!

HEEEEE OWOOOOO! HOOT HOOT!!

AïEEEEE YIP YIP HOOO HOOO HOOO!

3·5·3688

"B.A.A.A.A!"! LARRY YOU ARE SUCH A WAG!!

YE GODS! STANDARDS HAVE NOSE-DIVED SINCE I WAS AN EGG!

I'M GOING TO PUT A STOP TO THIS RIGHT NOW!! GET IN THAT SHED!

CRACK

WINSTON SPENCER CHURCHILL, SAVIOUR OF THE BRITISH WAY OF LIFE WAS BORN IN DRONE DRONE DRONE...

I CAN'T CONCENTRATE—THIS CLASS IS TOO SMALL!

©Steve Bell 1995

DECENCY.....

Prime Minister The Right Hon. John Major M.P.

—4·5·3689—

INTEGRITY...

HONESTY....

©Steve Bell 1995

BOLLOCKS...

5·5·3690—

©Steve Bell '95—

I'LL MEET AGAINNN.... DON'T KNOW WHERE DON'T KNOW WHEN

TAP

BUT I KNOW I'LL MEET AGAIN SOME SUNNY DAY....

FURQUE YOU SAATCHI! YOU DON' BUY MY SHEEPS — I GET EVEN WITH YOU!

DIPPED DAMIEN

© Steve Bell 1995

DEAD DIPPED DAMIEN

DISSECTED DEAD DIPPED DAMIEN

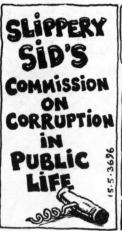

SLIPPERY SID'S COMMISSION ON CORRUPTION IN PUBLIC LIFE

15·5·3696

ITEM ONE: APPOINTMENTS TO THE QUANGO TO OVERSEE APPOINTMENTS TO QUANGOS......

© Steve Bell '95

DRINKS

WHAT AM I BID??

FIFTEEN QUID! MY MUM!

A PINT, A PIE AND A FRIENDLY WORD — MY BUTLER!

GET REAL! WE WANT SOMEONE WITH CLOUT, NOT YOUR MUM OR YOUR BUTLER!

RUPERT BEAR!

DAVID MELLOR!

I NOMINATE THE PERSON FORMERLY KNOWN AS PRINCE CHARLES!

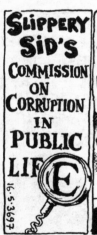

SLIPPERY SID'S COMMISSION ON CORRUPTION IN PUBLIC LIFE

16·5·3697

ANY BUNG OVER FIVE THOUSAND QUID SHOULD AUTOMATICALLY BE TREATED AS A PERSONAL PENSION CONTRIBUTION.

© Steve Bell '95

THIS MEASURE SHOULD OPTIMISE TAX-EFFICIENCY FOR THE POTENTIAL BUNGEE

HEAR HEAR!

LONG OVERDUE!

M.P.s SHOULD NOT BE EMPLOYED BY LOBBYING FIRMS...

GASP!

THAT'S RADICAL!

LOBBYING FIRMS SHOULD BE CALLED SOMETHING ELSE IN ORDER TO SPARE M.P.s' BLUSHES!

HOW ABOUT 'ETHICS MONITORS'?

THAT'S ONLY SENSIBLE

SLIPPERY SID'S COMMISSION ON CORRUPTION IN PUBLIC LIFE

13·5·3698

SOLD

HERE YOU ARE, WAITING WORLD — HERE ARE SLIPPERY SID'S EIGHT PRINCIPLES OF PUBLIC LIFE:

① SELFLESSNESS
② INTEGRITY
③ OBJECT-IVITY
④ ACCOUNTABILITY
⑤ OPENNESS
⑥ HONESTY
⑦ LEADERSHIP
⑧ BOL-LURCKS

© Steve Bell 1995

156

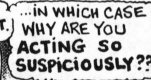